REAPER'S MILONGA

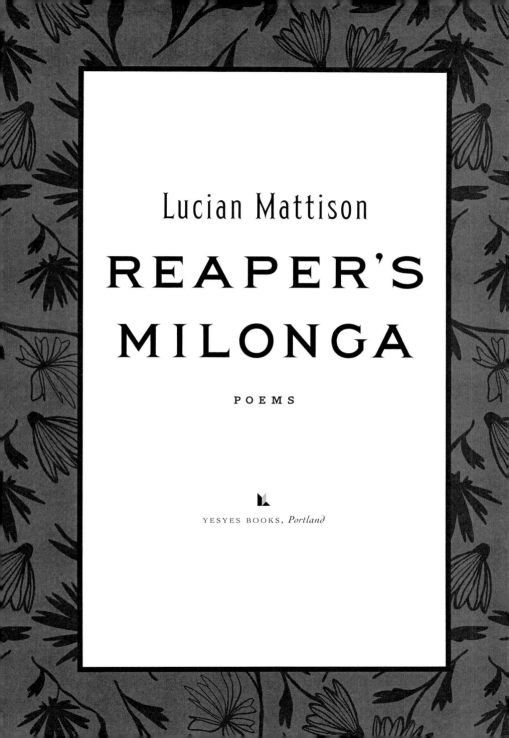

Lucian Mattison

REAPER'S MILONGA

POEMS

YESYES BOOKS, *Portland*

REAPER'S MILONGA © 2018 BY LUCIAN MATTISON

COVER ART: "MARGARITAS" PATTERN DESIGN BY DARLIN & CO.

INTERIOR ART: "MOCKING BIRD DRAGGING UP A PAST LIFE"

©2009 BY MATTHEW BOYLE

COVER & INTERIOR DESIGN: ALBAN FISCHER

ISBN 978-1-936919-54-3

PRINTED IN THE UNITED STATES OF AMERICA

THIS IS A LIMITED EARLY PRINT RUN

AVAILABLE ONLY FROM AUTHOR AND YESYES BOOKS

PUBLISHED BY YESYES BOOKS

1614 NE ALBERTA ST

PORTLAND, OR 97211

YESYESBOOKS.COM

KMA SULLIVAN, PUBLISHER

JOANN BALINGIT, ASSISTANT EDITOR

STEVIE EDWARDS, SENIOR EDITOR, BOOK DEVELOPMENT

ALBAN FISCHER, GRAPHIC DESIGNER

COLE HILDEBRAND, SENIOR EDITOR OF OPERATIONS

JILL KOLONGOWSKI, MANAGING EDITOR

BEYZA OZER, DEPUTY DIRECTOR OF SOCIAL MEDIA

AMBER RAMBHAROSE, CREATIVE DIRECTOR OF SOCIAL MEDIA

CARLY SCHWEPPE, ASSISTANT EDITOR, *VINYL*

PHILLIP B. WILLIAMS, COEDITOR IN CHIEF, *VINYL*

AMIE ZIMMERMAN, EVENTS COORDINATOR

HARI ZIYAD, ASSISTANT EDITOR, *VINYL*

Contents

REAPER'S MILONGA

Gin Gang Milonga

It follows the slug of bell tongue,
rattle against the apple
of an ox throat. Hoof after
hoof, breath chuffed,
is this how we are all yoked?
Death steps a tight circle
maintains the image of moving
forward, always pulling in
closer to the center
of this ancient structure,
lugging the rotation
of our hearts. It pulls in worship,
interminable ring of filling
its own fresh hoofprints, lifetime
spent dancing atop hay rot —
palpably wet, overwhelming.

Goring

Maybe you saw me in the Picasso Museum,
how I stood for an hour in front of *Gored Horse*
thinking about Plaza de Toros in Pamplona

praying to the toro lidiado, how banderillas
dripped a rosary of blood down its obsidian pelt.
Yes, the grandstand was full. No, women

did not beg for the bull's ears when it finally stumbled.
The beast leaned against corrugated iron
catching its breath to the chagrin of spectators.

The torero was ushered off stage, tail tucked
between his legs. Birds glittering above, their little razor-
blade wings cut sheet music on cerulean dusk.

Nothing about it was torturous, indeterminate;
it was chaines turns and feather steps until the goring.
Nobody won. When their bodies came together,

it only made sense: head upswept,
costumed body twirled on a horizontal axis,
horn the choreographer of blooding. It could be

I confuse sex with what is worthy of worship,
but in that museum I ran my tongue
along the deckle fringe of the bull's severed tail,

my body a banderilla thrust in reverence.
I was worshipping the arena in which we injure,
watch worn partners bleed before us.

Pintura Negra

— *After Francisco Goya's "Saturn Devouring His Son"*

We follow the porcelain
column of a child's arm

into time's mouth, desperate
Titan, runnel of inked tear

spilling from his eye.
This feels like the beginning

of knowing death. It digs
nails into the small

of a child's back, white-
knuckled grip of a father

arthritic from holding
dead things. The whole scene

weeps a blurred body,
brings a child into the world

embalmed by the deaf. Death
and artist, two skulking

lumps, billow canvas curtain.
These are the ghosts

that move marrow, fingers
that slip the knife point

into a notch of soft bone,
and lift the broken end

to our lips to drink
this dark paint that fills us.

Taking Death as a Lover

He says the physics
baffle him, but that's precisely
what makes it so hot.

Death is the type of lover
you fuck standing up.
Its cloaked nothingness

only hovers as if
inflated, its breath a head
of cold wind in the grip

of a cinched hood.
He says sex with Death
is like finding oneself

stuck neck deep
in a frozen lake.
He blindly thrusts,

attempts to penetrate
the absence in the cowl,
shroud enveloping his body.

The seconds before Death's
brittle orgasm
it cries, *We're dying!*

We're dying! He confirms,
it's true,
it's actually like dying

or heroin,
but as far as he can tell,
he's coming into a towel.

He says because of Death's
whole situation, they can't share
tender moments — no kiss

on the neck as he washes
dishes, no lovemaking
atop an open map,

cordillera spread like sheets —
Death just asks that he carry
its bundled bones

against his chest. Palms up,
gentle cup around the clack
of its light weight,

he says embracing Death
is like hugging a burlap sack
of limp ibis. Death is too old to walk

for itself, but loves to go
to the beach to *take it all in.*
Most days, at first light,

he pulls Death's skull out
at the shore, kisses
the polished marble, and points

its sockets out toward the dark
water, inviting his baptism
in the sea foam.

In Search of Sheep

The first pope I saw
was the toy in a glass

box, traveling faith, bullet
proof as it glided along pavement.

His reach extended as far as his nose
could sniff, his scent

filling the plate glass cage,
numbed touch, my tiny head

bowed beside my mother's
weeping mien, television

screen sweeping across crowds
of devoted. The pistol

was an old hat means of choosing
popes, the conclave for Saint

Peter an older
and bigger hat only trumped

by the one on the pope's head
and those dozens of others

touching brims at the Preakness.
In any case, I can deduce

that hats of such size are synonymous
with exceptional wealth,

whether spiritual or material,
it must be quite a strain on the neck.

Perhaps, that's why at one point
clergy members were encouraged

to use the papal gym,
where altar boys and laity spotted

for the crumpled little men,
helped lift dumbbells

over their shoulders,
tiny pope traps flexed, triangular

and rock hard like their faith
reflected back at them in the mirror.

When it came to exercise,
most popes were goalkeepers

as children, watching
the scramble of other kids

all intent on putting boot to ball.
If you ask popes

they will tell you how they enjoyed
the privilege of being the only ones

that could use their hands to keep
everyone else from enjoying themselves.

As everyone knows, popes
are very entertaining as they perform

their duties. They know many jokes
that start: a priest, a rabbi, and an atheist.

Not everyone enjoys them, though.
One pope was shot.

I guess it's pretty sad,
but they had another waiting in the wings.

At least, he enjoyed his tenure.
Recently, I heard the pope

was beginning his US tour,
and after thinking of Katy Perry's

forthcoming work, I set out
on this hunt in search of sheep —

maybe the shepherd. I only found
these old jokes about hats

and the Popemobile (a Humvee
Pancho likens to a sardine can),

and that he maintains
he hasn't got much to lose in death.

My mother still gets very emotional
when she sees the pope,

but that's more an Argentinean
pride thing. I guess I am proud

of his current manifestation.
Today, my Catholicism

is some antique savonarola
or chaise lounge I put in storage

because they make little sense
in a modern living room.

Until now, it never seemed evangelical
thrones gave half a shit

about the warming of heaven
or how to make those puffy clouds

inclusive for all,
even if it means a woman being author

of her own decisions,
or encouraging two life partners

to lovingly cuddle on said
plush chaise lounge. Optimism

is a strong suit of mine,
so I won't get carried away. My hope

rests in the thought that the flies
are leaving the lips of our dead popes

in search of fresh carcasses,
that the remains of our popes and clergy

are treated as such, just bones,
some tangled up

in the roots of an upturned tree,
faults and crimes

evidenced by the trauma
dealt on their skeletons,

and some placed in a wooden box
labeled *Well-Behaved Pope*,

and set aside so we can move on
to more important things.

Good Son

Pull out his tongue,
clip the molluskan

base, chewed bubble
gum, mortadella sandwiched

between thumb and
forefinger. Sewing the wet

muscle onto my tongue,
trace the back

sides of teeth, cheek
walls, taste years

of someone else's spit,
my mother's, an altar

cup of sacramental
wine, navy ship

departing harbor — salt
spray pools in the mouth.

I can hardly breathe,
tongues are so large.

I don't eat shad roe,
speak drawl and spit.

Mother is prying
my mouth open,

sees the second
tongue shy away,

grabs a hold of it,
before it slips back

inside my mouth.
She won't let me look

away, clutching my chin
between her thumb

and four fingers.
She wants me

to spit it out,
but it's already done.

Décimas: Death as Milonguero

It was banned for a good portion
of time after the coup, said Death
moved like immoralism, said
Death was rooted in distortion
of the purist red right notion
of country. Death would dance embraced
with revolutionaries, traipsed
too close with those Montoneros
for comfort. With the long truncheon
Ongania couldn't erase

Death from the country — the exiled
professor it was thought to be —
when the fact remained, truthfully,
Death had no political guile.
Its craft was of another style,
deep devotion to those living
on its crescent blade: the wheezing
bandoneon player now jobless,
Conti in Cuba regardless
of radicals disappearing,

and the sacks of bones still humming
milongas on hospital beds.
Death was the country's song instead,
the dirty war's cowled face dropping
bodies in the ocean, to rings
of rebels arranging explosives.
The exile became meaningless.
Death's close embrace smothered dancers,
breathed rime on lips seeking answers,
its leading hand a cold caress.

Table Setting During the Corralito

Buenos Aires, 2002

I start an apology,
$\qquad$ puddle of water on my lap
seeping into denim. He bends

down on one knee in front of me
coolly collects wet bills,
$\qquad$ knives, napkins,
$\qquad$ each lard pastry,
spilling from his fingers as he fills them.

I could swear everything was sterling
flatware, table set
$\qquad$ so when the cloth was pulled
from beneath it all,
we would hardly notice the culprit's hands.

My uncle held a stack of notes,
$\qquad$ bank account frozen,
life savings halved by the devaluation.

He approached the table where I sat,
$\qquad$ wryly asked,

With no more of your Yankee dollars behind me,
how much do you think I'm worth now?

Thousands

of provisional Lecop fanned out
in his hand — I said *millions*
keeping this cruel joke going.

He stuffed one bill
between his right cheek
and gums,
before slinging the rest in a billow
toward the dining room table
as if these worthless notes
burned his fingers.

I jerked my body back, pulled a cloth-wrapped
thigh and dragged
everything on the table away with me.

The water cup rolled onto my lap,
warm butter,
libritos, and dinnerware following
the procession of my leg
to the linoleum floor.

I'm sliding the cloth back into place,
as he sets our new table
                in the quilombo: two fistfuls

of objects released before me in a mound
for breakfast, and a cup
                suffocating upside down
        in a puddle of apology,
lips pressed to table.

Election Day

Cordoba, Argentina

If we woke to water rot,
fallen oak crossbeam
bisecting the breakfast table,

a nest of ants shattered
like a chandelier on tile,
I could hardly fault the architect.

They eat insulation, hollow
out the roof, bring water and mountain
cold with them. Each day

this month passes between
a condor's beak, strings
hours with a sewing needle.

The shopkeeper sells beef milanesa
by the yard, our neighbor's
son pisses in his lover's bed

and for the third time
blames the dog. Tio Carlos
keeps saying, *honesty*

is a jail cell, crooks the wardens,
as election ads preen television screens
with images of grandmothers,

rolling Pampa. We feel ants
crawl among the hairs
on our ankles as he smokes

two cigarettes in two minutes,
kisses me on the cheek
as if I were a toddler. We mark

the calendar for every day
the ants come back, tick today's box,
boil a pot of water

to pour between the rafters,
knowing full well
of the damage the solution demands —

how it smokes in spring
like false fire on the tin.
We each grip a pot

with oven mitts. He climbs the ladder,
crooks the wardens,
under his breath. Boiling

water rolls over the eaves
like sheet glass. A thin line scorches
a perimeter surrounding the house

as if slowly cutting us out
of the country like a ripped elbow patch,
dead ants in lines.

Moving Homes

I pat my pockets, dull outline
of what I carry, key ring
and wallet like furniture

draped in a dim living room.
My touch is linen, a ticket away,
the morning an open window

from which a fat turtle
pokes its head. The simple act
of walking outside feels like defiance.

I've known this home three years,
unremarkable town, and now
I hold a sprig of mint

to nostalgia's nose, lead it
just out of jaw's reach,
neck stretching as if I could draw

the creature out of itself
like a brain pulled through the nostril
before the embalming.

We've done this before,
sold ourselves on expectation, paper
currency we accept, smiling.

We circulate perceived worth
from hand to hand,
to breakfast table — tomorrow

the cup of blackberries
atop a dish of crème fraiche.
I hold a new city like a wad of bills,

hand undiscerning
of the counterfeit.
When it comes to this brand of faith

isn't it better not to question?
Boxes arranged in the bed
of my pickup, I close myself

inside its tortoise shell;
I fill my mouth with copper coins
so I don't need to speak.

Death in Venice

Even after hundreds of years of plagues
and oaths of revenge calling it into action,

Death won't set foot on a gondola
not because it's self-conscious

about fitting the boatman stereotype
so obviously, but that Death always feared

open water, deemed it the most effective barrier
between here and the afterlife —

this, of course, before the advent of galleons
and triathlon swimmers — and this city

was a perfect marriage of two realms,
a place where humans might try to understand

the glaring duality present in their existence.
Death is at home, can lay its scythe down,

put its feet up, and watch from afar
as humans move through time

like briskly dipped oars, as if in a rush
to meet it at the shore, or attempting

to dethrone its natural order.
Perhaps this answers Death's questions

about the human race's proclivity
for pedophilia, just another desperate effort

at retaining some semblance of youth.
But that's not why Death came today.

Death is in Venice because it wants to remember
the feeling of being between

the columns of the Piazza San Marco,
where so many took its hand

at the moment of their execution.
It wants to feel the tinge of nostalgia

ticker in its bones before the city finally sinks.
It wants to stand proud like the lion, no,

like San Teodoro, feet on the dragon's back,
scythe pointed to the heavens

to curse the world for drowning
this city so wealthy in death.

Imagine the solitude in the flooded square,
the lack of meaning where the criminal's fingers

no longer reach out for Death's hand,
no more ecstasy at the climax

of touching finger to absence.
But is not nothingness a form

of perfection? Death quotes to itself.
Yes, of course it is. As is the world of water

which takes a city and all of its inhabitants,
a place never to be open to the whims

of reaping again. Why the obsession
with humans, Death asks itself, why

must it continue to give itself to them
without the slightest hint of reciprocation.

Death lowers its cowl, rolls up its sleeves
and stands between the two pillars.

Bracing itself, it pushes outward
wishing to die here with the common humans

so it may feel the perfection
it promises the dying. And Death waits.

And nothing moves,
nothing collapses onto its cloaked presence,

nothing crushes its bones into meal,
and nothing could be more sad.

How to Better Mourn

There's always finger food
after a funeral, tasty cakes

and the like, but nobody's
wrapping dinner rolls in napkins

so I fill mine, bulk up my chest
and thigh pockets. Sure,

my refrigerator has become a bag
of baby carrots, old chimichurri,

the door full to the gunwales
with capless condiment bottles.

A third straight cold shower
means the boiler is empty of oil

and I can't be bothered
to fill it up — I'm not pretending

any longer that I know how
to handle important things

like money or death — shivering
hands cupped to my chest,

they fill up with glassy weight
until I let these cold wave

packets of bathwater fall
to my claw foot tub bowl,

dense slap resounding
in the metal for a pleasing second,

petering out just as quickly.
This seems to me

like a small form of death;
the same applies to falling asleep

with food in the oven, spilled
beer bottle as bedmate.

Do we all wake up thinking
we've pissed the bed?

Does anyone else smell something
burning? In Indonesia,

when someone dies they tether
a chicken to a stick, erect

the setup near the crematorium
because they believe its head

is a sponge drinking in malicious
ghosts that always seem to loiter

when we burn bodies.
I try not to wear death's feathers

like a cape. Instead I hold
my mouth open to its rising ash,

but this doesn't feel like wisdom.
Keeping evil spirits

inside a pet hen seems
like a better way of mourning.

You don't even have to eat the thing.
If you let it, it will keep laying

egg after egg after egg —

Homunculus

In my mouth   a heart beats
fly wings around my chest,
          spills fruit juice
down my chin.   I feel the impossibility
of previous months spent thinking

I could grow alone,
          unhinged from a lover,
my image knocking dumbly about
in a glass of tap water

by my bedside.   I've tried to be a head
wrapped tight

in the sepals of sleep,
                    remaining closed
at the end of a leaf node —

But today a new lover leaves my flat
in the morning, and I dive

                    headfirst into the pit
of a drupe, my burrowing tongue
trying to reenter her origin. I carry

her idea in me, cored desire.
                    My stomach fills,

        a drop of sugared water,
mango in my right hand
                    the rain
gathered at the point of a leaf —
                    waiting for it
to reach its critical mass — inevitable
drip, my consciousness

a seed stuck with toothpicks, hovering
half-submerged in a glass. Alone

I grow a peeling mask,
contrived, unaware
        I'm drowning
in my own liquids. I thought I could grow

desire in an empty home, the sun
enough to sprout leaves
                    from bone marrow,

but I only see a bare balcony, a smaller man
looking out. I offer myself

                    to my lover, again

in my bedroom, because what I let open
                somehow opens wider
than the limits of the bloom, panicles

branched like veins of her inner thigh
and wrists, these thousands
of ways leading back to the heart.

Making Bucatini

From cracked shells, two yolks
        nestle in the pocket
of bleached flour — whisking
        these two elements
into one another with a fork.
        Your hands on
the wine bottle, stopgap
        rolling pin, you hum a melody
like scattered flour
        over the countertop.

Look at these improper tools
        I've used my whole life,
how none of it matters
        when you pick up
the bottle we emptied
        the previous night,
and roll it across the dough —
        my amniotic living
you knead into something solid —
        how it expands
by way of another's hands.

Tooth

Rattlesnake Creek, FL

At first, you said no
when I told you
I found taillights, halves
of soda cans, weathered

glass in the creek —
how one time I kicked
a water moccasin
out of a sunken car radiator,

as if this were a surefire way
of convincing you
to come. I thought
it would never happen,

until you asked me
if I was free. It was June,
I was jobless,
and you were the one

asking. From the car
door to the river,

we were the kind of quiet
that stutters inside

an idling engine.
We dragged our feet
upstream through braids
of water, ankles

like fallen branches
carving rifts in the flow.
We stopped at deposits,
shallow gradients

where we could read
the stream over a pillow,
where the shark teeth
collect. Our knees dug

into the riverbed,
mosquitoes latched
onto arms, our hands
pleasure-curled

calices. We lifted
fistfuls of sediment,
fingers sweeping,
straining, sieves

picking out teeth:
fossilized ray, serrated
edges of prehistoric
tiger sharks —

remnants of a time
when this whole state
was a hidden landmass,
rising up from the sea.

When the sun folded over
the canopy line,
I lifted a white shark's
tooth from beneath

a paint can lid, fossil
as tall as a thumb,
crown from wet shale,
broad chevron

decorating the base
with a stripe
of Miocene perfection.
We ran fingertips

over ridges, primal
texture, nothing

I'd ever touched before.
Feet sunk in the mud

of that afternoon,
our nerves wet
clothes shed
on the stream bank,

you spilled over me
in silt. I held
what felt like millions
of years converging

in one place —
your right hand.
I set the tooth
in your palm

like it was fate,
blank space on a map
of this county
that only we could fill.

Stick and Poke Tattoo

He sets a black chess

        rook aflame

in a ceramic bowl

        stirs ashes with vodka

into homemade tattoo ink

        retraces the fading

        ink retraces

        the faded line

a second year

        of scrawl down his leg

he knows the needle point

coarse poke

like pubic hair

on thighs

cold boxcar

metal to skin

where thousand mile

paper slips

away slips away

by stick and poke

he hems

a strange curve

down thigh skin

inscribes a timeline

memory of her hands

guiding the needle

years that follow

this scar's endless

drip blood and ink since

she last left

since she last

left he burns

a chess rook

royal into carbon

black ash ounce

of vodka its carrier

two years retracing

extending this thread

single cord pricked

down his left leg

a lifeline

a fishhook

a question mark

depending on the day

Ash Wednesday

I am the same boy
in the morning
who looks into the rolling boil.
Eggs buoying
in a saucepan, I whisper
the *Padre Nuestro*
three times, as they dance
to a soft running
yolk. My phone
lights up beside
the cutting board,
a text from a coworker —
her sick husband in rehab —
she writes, *our God is*
a great God. The words
I pocket in my slacks,
repeat to myself to feel
how they poke
perforations in my head
like fork tines through
solid oil. How fitting
the absence that just appears

in a life — after childhood,
we hold onto the divine
in the same way
the widower fluffs a pillow
for the passed —
and years later,
this absence is replaced
with another, emptier one,
as if fixing this glaring hole
made in us
were as easy as patching
the roof with a photograph
of a different hole.

I crack the egg top
with the back of a spoon,
a shell cup of half cooked yolk
after prayer. The methodical
triviality of tradition
burned into me
pushes the minute hand
forward, the spoon to my lips.
My grandmother's
instruction for huevitos
pasados por agua
feels like baptism in the boil
of the morning commute.
And of course, today, downtown

is pockmarked with charcoal

crosses. The odd three

people in the crowd

of the train's dozens

wear an antique

smudged on their forehead.

In their sleepy eyes,

I recognize a whole

realm of former self.

My skin unmarked, I

with they, ask

in our own ways

for deliverance. My afterlife

a part of my past,

I keep the dead

at the beginning,

foundation on which I am

built, mausoleum

on marmoreal face,

hardened by God, never again

between the friction

ridges of a priest's finger.

To 30

A dog joins the neighborhood's
chorus of more baying
dogs at front gates,
unsure of why this all started
and why it joined in.

In a rental, I open
the flue before autumn,
call up the tower
to nobody. A muffle, nearly
an echo, climbs
bricks, escapes
into the wind without a trace.

Think of it this way:

The previous year
hungrily spooned out
clumps of quinoa like red
ants from a stockpot,
colony in miniature

hovering between the tines
of a fork.

The previous year
sat facing its partner, nude
on the bathroom floor.
Its fingers swam into her,
beckoning the condom
that slipped off.

The previous year wished
to clone previous years
like rosemary, root fleshy
sprigs in adjunct soil.
I am now digging

at the front gate.
Loose grains tumble in
from all sides, refilling
what I've started.
With each handful
I create negative
space, an image
of movement where
there is no object at all.

Music School for the Dying

The instructor begins each class
by humiliating those students stubborn enough
to choose electric guitar over a woodwind,

then plucks acetate transparencies
covering music theory on and off
the overhead projector with its bone fingers.

From beneath its cowl, the instructor moans
painful demonstrations of microtonal
compositions, and as usual,

the woodblock students giggle and knock elbows,
the jazz band doesn't give one single fuck
about respect for the dead

or scaffolded instruction,
and the germophobe bassoonists strictly compose
on paper, their double reeds abandoned

since traveling from oboe to horn,
and between everybody else's lips.
The jazz band claims it's always raining inside

the building when they sound at all subpar,
sling mouthpieces and crumpled worksheets
at the instructor's turned back,

before returning to their endless serenade
of themselves. Still,
the instructor always applauds

after each sax solo and gestures wildly
with its scythe as if to show the class
that improvisation and self efficacy

might mean something terribly important
to those still living. Most have chosen
to play woodblock, and for no good reason

other than a passing grade. The instructor
rarely acknowledges the two-toned chorus
of slit-drum *clacks* and *tocks*

until a number of students die of natural causes
and the room starts to smell.
For some, recess means silent prayer.

Others prefer to expend all of their energy
yelling questions at death's empty cloak.
There are also swing sets.

When the bell rings again,
students gather in the auditorium
for the mandatory MacBook DJ set workshops,

and wedding and bar mitzvah host training
(a hard science). The rest of the afternoon
is dedicated to personal compositions

and practice in windowless rooms.
As the day comes to a close,
tuning forks are struck, instruments packed,

and the instructor opens its cloak
exposing students to the indefinite absence within,
so those unwilling or too tired to go on

may climb inside. The class
is then whisked over to St. Burchardi church
for the daily field trip.

The instructor likes to remind them
of their pending mortality
in the face of the 639-year-long composition —

also, that John Cage was a real person
who did common things
like shake his pedometer to simulate exercise.

Whether in silence or amid the steady one-note
drone inside the cathedral,
the instructor feels "As Slow as Possible"

helps define the idea of death to students
in the post-apocalyptic terms which obsess them all.
They listen, describe the hymn's monotony:

fracture of concrete spilling over piles of more
concrete, teeth cracking boiled bones
of mysterious origin to tap marrow,

the inherent song within a sustained rest —
scavenger holding its breath in the brush
as it waits for the hunter to abandon its kill.

Seeking God Midflight

We remember thinking angels
slept on the top sides
of clouds, that heaven
was the wool
blanket swaddling earth
where it was coldest.

After countless window seats
and fogged up panes,
the tip of our noses
grew numb
on the glass enough times
to know nobody
was that good

at hiding. Grasping
odds, infinitude of planets
better suited for us
than our own,
we now ask where
else could heaven be
but outer space — God

in broken supersymmetry,
His mouth closed
for good around stars
and billions of us
embering in His throat

before the exhale?
It's not right,
all of this waiting
for something to lift
the vast loneliness
that mantles
our universe.

Why expect anything
to arrive millennia
too late to tell us
there is an opening
that breathes
on the fringes of our galaxy?

Circumambient

Today she appears in a blue mantle,
knitted white stars all over her sweater.

She grips a lamppost while on her phone,
unconsciously paces circles around the pole

as if yoked — Arm a radius,
body endlessly turning inward.

For a half hour, I watch her pulled
by her core, impossibly magnetic,

and I'm reminded of wanting
someone with my whole being

the way I could when I was younger —
From a distance, never exchanging a word

with my desire. I still have yet to break
from this world of watching,

how the expanse in front of me
is actually the distending of my own chest,

distance between people more
a measurement of how small our worlds are.

And today I watch, kid again,
trying to disappear with someone

into imagined space,
a telephone receiver, her mouth,

labyrinth of her ear. I imagine her
walking into my bedroom — Drunk

between her legs, the whole world
one temperature; we are tenon

fit into mortise wearing each other's
wordless skins through sleep.

The morning watches her dress
in the cold just beyond the covers.

I place my ear to the front door,
listen to her heels strike the staircase

as she leaves, her phantom
sighs lingering over the mattress.

I peel back another layer of myself,
and I can't help but think I've been drinking

from this type of woman ever since I slipped
the womb, hit ground, and hoisted

up the whole earth when standing
that first time — My planet

of a head pulled by its iron core, loving
those I keep only close enough to steal me

into orbit. It's clockwork, my desire
to be this dumb object for a woman —

How maybe it's not the idea
of intimacy, but dedication

to only one person that lets me know
nobody wants to be a moon

slipping from a planet's clutch,
inches farther every year.

The longer I watch this woman,
the more I find myself wanting

to open my apartment window,
ask her if it's possible

to exist in two places at once,
our bodies separated by volumes

of space, heads binary objects
dependent on our cislunar distance,

ears strung through the middle
by invisible cord.

And if she would answer me,
I could tell her I'm the one

she truly longs to be with
and away from at once — Boson

to her fermion — theories of one another
like shadows commingling

in another reality. I can almost hear my voice
on the other end of her phone.

Duende

She knows it well,
birth starting
deformity in motion
beneath skin, the clouds
turned sacks of rice
on her shoulders.
Her spine bends
like cheap silverware
against fingers.
Mouth on mine,
she sings a contract
into us, life
a column curling
ribs into the heart.
I hear a faint spell
of church chime
in her bones,
tongue-struck
funeral bell trickling
irregular melody
down her back.
I make love

to her early
departure, keep vigil
as I trace her legs
like the walls
of an unlit room,
always reaching
for the origin,
an absent switch
on her hip.

Paper Skirts

What if I painted
nudes — visions
of women, pale and dark
haired: one hunched
over her laptop
on the coffee table,
asleep on a black couch
swallowing her whole,
or belly up in bed
surrounded by unpacked
boxes — would you search
each face for another,
feel the acid of ex-lovers
like a peach pit
rooted in the lining
of your stomach? I say
the image of a woman
is just that, image,
whether whispered
over a pillow or caked
in layers of acrylic.
I tell you people

from our past are just paper
skirts casting shadows
across the scrim
of our heads.
You know who we are
today couldn't be
without the cascade
behind us, months foaming
at a river's mouth, our eyes
two wet stones
looking out at the world
from sweet water.
I record years
for the sake of meaning,
but for you each old thought
of mine is paper
thin, a cut between
the fingers, meaningless
hurt, inescapably present.
You tell me this
in the car, seat belts on,
the idle breathing beneath us.
We lean to kiss
in the darkness of the garage,
against the harness
strapping us to our places,
necks outstretched,
unguarded.

After Closing Shift

Wring out the rag
of my body, relieve me
of these clothes,

every frayed bit
this tired garment
twisting in your grip.

Hold me above
your mouth. Let me drip
onto your tongue.

Drink all of me in,
my body unraveled
muslin sheets. Climb

onto the pomanders
of my parted lips. Close
your eyes with me.

Milonguero

Rolled-up, wrinkled
               shirts and student debt,
    the third time this year,
    my torso
is an open suitcase, lungs,
                  stomach carelessly
stuffing me like warm laundry.

    Zipped up, I walk out
              on the last two payments
of a rental, empty it all out
onto another
           wooden floor.
Every room is always too large.
             It fastens me to the thought
    that the less a person carries
the shorter distance traveled
              between action and the heart —

that I could keep shrinking
              every aspect of my life

         starting with the apartment walls,
until I'm only a series of dance
              steps, craft and passion,
              locked in a tight embrace.

*

At the core, desire truly is
       this simple — sensation
       of ice water left
              on my partner's lips
when she returns to bed,

a natural, smaller room
           fulfilled in the mouth,
a body filled by taste, solid
             clarity, and cold —

and need is being
          without water,
days spent outdoors   sleeping back to tree
     roots, under canvas
     roofs, raindrops that tap
     the tongue too little
             to sate — all proof
pointing to how common we actually are,
animals in search

                    of water, our memory
an impression of bodies on the grass
where we last slept.

                    *

Months later, I am again turning   a key,
entering a new, smaller room,   sparse

like I've let go of too much,
                    mistaken deprivation
for happiness, let the bedlam
                    of mountain valley root
          beneath the floorboards.
                              The ceiling fan

          swirls clouds, my sun
the immutable bulb
                    as I wait for the filament
to burn out.

                    Life reduced to what I can carry
on my back, I peel the finish
                    off of the floorboards
and pocket it, as if to somehow assign meaning
to my skin,

                    to justify its worth.

                    *

I ask my partner,

                after our debts are settled,

if our heads are enough, everything

                that a human should carry

on their shoulders until the world

                finally goes dark?

She is asleep, wrapped in blankets.

                On her face,

        I see our silent capital,

                weightlessness in dance:

how we approach the rubble of our future,

                post-apocalyptic city,

      concrete spilled along the ground

like cold laundry.

                In silence,

I stack books on the floor

            beside her breathing, warm

        my throat over the flame

of a plastic lighter — in all of this

                sustained quiet, this movement

and two voices

            are the only kind of glow

        heard for miles.

Acknowledgments

Grateful acknowledgment is made to the following publications in which some of these poems appeared: *The Adroit Journal* ("Tooth"); *apt* ("In Search of Sheep"); *Barely South Review* ("Duende"); *The Bitter Oleander* ("Gin Gang Milonga," "Pintura Negra"); *The Boiler* ("After Closing Shift"); *Cleaver Magazine* ("Homunculus"); *Four Way Review* ("Stick and Poke Tattoo"); *Hobart* ("Circumambient,"); *Midway Journal* ("How to Better Mourn"); *Nashville Review* ("Moving Homes"); *Noctua Review* ("Seeking God Midflight"); *Poetry Quarterly* ("Making Bucatini"); *Powder Keg Magazine* ("Good Son," "Taking Death as a Lover"); *Puerto Del Sol* Poetry Prize Winner ("Election Day"); *Valparaiso Review* ("Goring").

Special thanks to my mentors Luisa Igloria, Remica Bingham-Risher, and Tim Seibles. Many thanks to Michael Alessi, Matt Boyle, Mark Cugini, Denise and Eric Geraldo-Gordon, Nick Gripp, Maha Haddad, Julia Hon, Katy Hurston, Tom Kelly, Mohamad Koubeissi, Sam Mahone, Chris Maier, Shannon and Tony Mancus, Joanie LG Parnell, Andrew Squitiro, Gloria Squitiro, Tara Squitiro, Caleb True, and KMA for being there to help this book come to life.

The utmost thanks to my brother, sister, and my parents for their endless love and support.

Argentinean-US poet and translator **LUCIAN MATTISON** is the author of two books of poetry, *Reaper's Milonga* (YesYes Books, 2018) and *Peregrine Nation* (Dynamo Verlag, 2017). His poetry, short fiction, and translations appear in numerous journals including *Hayden's Ferry Review*, *Hobart*, *Muzzle*, *Nano Fiction*, *The Nashville Review*, *The Offing*, *Puerto del Sol*, *Waxwing*, and is featured on poets.org. He is based out of DC and edits poetry for *Big Lucks*.

Also from YesYes Books

[insert] boy by Danez Smith

Man vs Sky by Corey Zeller

The Bones of Us by J. Bradley [Art by Adam Scott Mazer]

CHAPBOOK COLLECTIONS

VINYL 45S

After by Fatimah Asghar

Inside My Electric City by Caylin Capra-Thomas

Dream with a Glass Chamber by Aricka Foreman

Pepper Girl by Jonterri Gadson

Of Darkness and Tumbling by Mónica Gomery

Bad Star by Rebecca Hazelton

Makeshift Cathedral by Peter LaBerge

Still, the Shore by Keith Leonard

Please Don't Leave Me Scarlett Johansson by Thomas Patrick Levy

Juned by Jenn Marie Nunes

A History of Flamboyance by Justin Phillip Reed

No by Ocean Vuong

This American Ghost by Michael Wasson

BLUE NOTE EDITIONS

Beastgirl & Other Origin Myths by Elizabeth Acevedo

Kissing Caskets by Mahogany L. Browne

One Above One Below: Positions & Lamentations by Gala Mukomolova

COMPANION SERIES

Inadequate Grave by Brandon Courtney

The Rest of the Body by Jay Deshpande